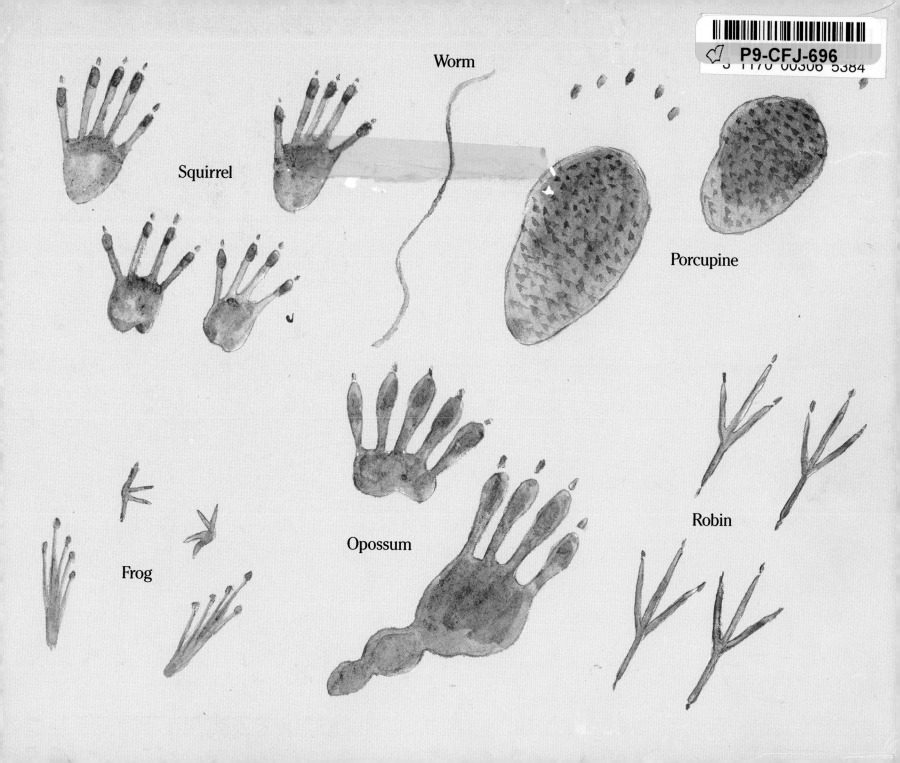

Squirrel

Worm

Porcupine

Opossum

Frog

Robin

Animal Tracks

To Amanda, Lily, Ethan, and Alex

Library of Congress Cataloging-in-Publication Data

Dorros, Arthur.
Animal tracks/written and illustrated by Arthur Dorros.
p.   cm.
Summary: Introduces the tracks and signs left by various animals, including the raccoon, duck, frog, black bear, and human.
ISBN 0-590-43367-9
1. Animal tracks — Juvenile literature. [1. Animal tracks.] I. Title.
QL768.D67   1991
591—dc20   90-21269
                                                                        CIP
                                                                         AC

12 11 10 9 8 7 6 5 4 3 2   2 3 4 5 6/9

Printed in the U.S.A.   36

First Scholastic printing, November 1991

Designed by Anna DiVito

The illustrations in this book are watercolor and ink paintings.

Animal Tracks

Written and illustrated by
Arthur Dorros

j 591.5
DOR

SCHOLASTIC
HARDCOVER

SCHOLASTIC INC.
New York

When you go into the forest, the animals may be hiding. But you can tell which animals are in the forest by looking at their tracks.

Who made tracks in the soft mud by the stream?

A raccoon was looking for food.
Look out, crayfish, or you will be the raccoon's breakfast!

Who made tracks from the reeds to the water?

A family of ducks waddled from their nest in the reeds.

But who made tracks even smaller than
the ducklings' feet?

A frog made the tracks as it hopped along
with small front feet and bigger hind feet.

A turtle is warming up in the sun.
Who made tracks almost as big as the turtle?

A deer walked to the stream to drink.

Some of the tracks are not easy to see.
Where an animal stepped on hard ground, rocks, or plants
there may be no tracks, or only part of a track.

Who scared the deer and made tracks
up the stream bank?

A fox chased a rabbit along the stream bank.

Where the rabbit ran, the tracks are far apart.
The rabbit hopped far with each jump.
The rabbit made it home this time.

The fox looks at her reflection in a puddle.
Whose tracks are curving lines in the mud
around the puddle?

A worm is slithering along.
Watch out, worm. Watch out, cricket!
A bird is hopping, looking for a meal.

Nearby is a tree that looks as if it has been chewed.
Who eats trees for lunch?

A porcupine ate tree bark until she was full.
Then she walked slowly away.
Porcupines don't have to move fast.
Who would bother a porcupine?

The black bear won't bother the porcupine.
He is busy eating berries.

Then he will rub and scratch on his favorite tree.
The scratches show that he has been there.
The scratches are called a "sign."

Who left another animal sign — teeth marks
on a fallen tree?

A beaver chewed the tree to cut it down.
Beavers drag branches away to build their
round lodge home and a beaver dam.
Behind the dam is a beaver pond.

Who lives among the tall grasses by the beaver pond?

A heron looks for fish to eat.
Muskrats are eating grass.
They leave a sign — a raft of chewed grass
floating in the water.

SLAP! A beaver's tail hits the water,
warning of danger.
Who is making crackling noises in the bushes
by the pond?

A dog runs along a trail, followed by people.
Each person leaves a different-sized track.
There are small tracks and larger tracks
made by small feet and larger feet.

Near a lake are tracks made in sand by bare feet.
Along the road there are muddy tire tracks.
A car is going toward a city.

Cities can be good places to find animal tracks.

Listen carefully, and look for animal signs.
Snow, soft sand, mud, and dust are good places
to look for tracks.

You might even find tracks of animals
that can live in cities, but usually stay hidden —
raccoons, muskrats, or opossums.
Once people even found mountain lion tracks
in a city park!

Be a track detective.
Guess who made *these* tracks in a city park?

Here's how to collect tracks to look at again later:

Plaster casts —

You can use plaster of paris or water putty (from the hardware store; used for patching cracks). Find some tracks. Mix the powder with water until it is about the thickness of applesauce. As soon as it's mixed, pour carefully into tracks. Let it harden (about ten to twenty minutes), then lift it out carefully. Dirt can be rinsed or brushed off gently with an old toothbrush.

Tracings or drawings —

If tracks are dry, put a piece of tracing paper (paper you can see through) over them. Then trace or cut around the tracks. If the tracks are wet (in mud, wet sand, or snow) you can sketch them. Measuring can help in remembering how big the tracks were.

Track "traps" —

Spread a coating of flour, baking soda, or other powder on dry ground in an area about as wide as your arms spread out. Place some bait: either nuts, peanut butter, vegetables, fruit, or bread, in the center of your "trap." Leave the trap overnight, and come back and see who has been visiting. You can trace or draw the tracks to save them.

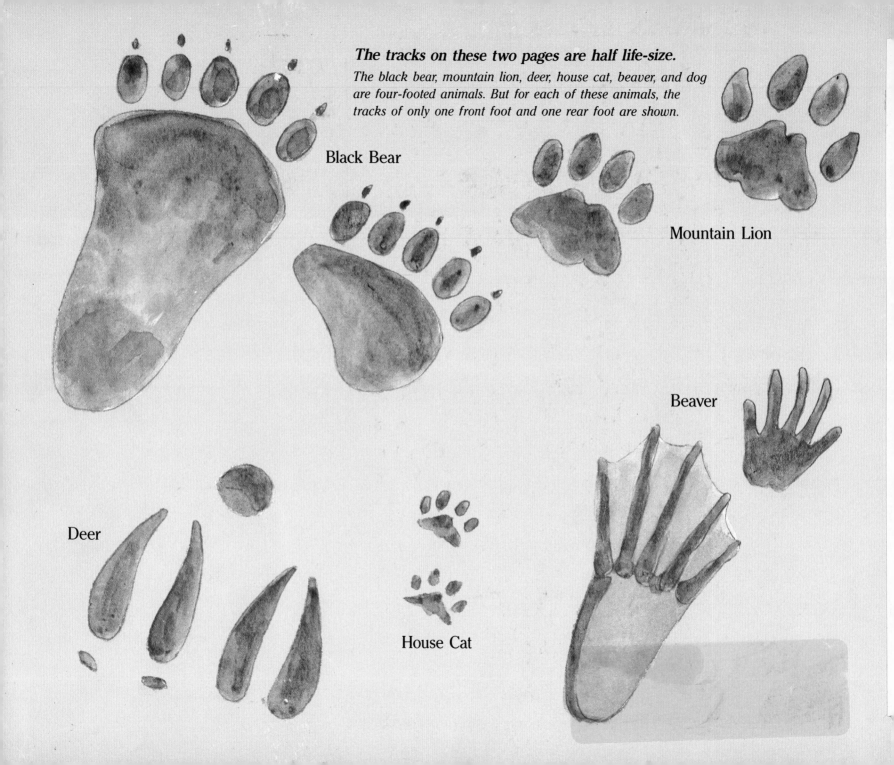

The tracks on these two pages are half life-size.

The black bear, mountain lion, deer, house cat, beaver, and dog are four-footed animals. But for each of these animals, the tracks of only one front foot and one rear foot are shown.

Black Bear

Mountain Lion

Beaver

Deer

House Cat